GLORIOUS
FRUIT
DESSERTS

Consultant Editor:
Valerie Ferguson

HH
HERMES
HOUSE

Contents

Introduction

There is something special about the first strawberries of the summer and the first crisp apples of the autumn. While supermarkets provide an astonishing array of fresh fruit all year round, nothing tastes quite so wonderful or succulent as newly ripened fruits in season.

Raw fruit is the perfect snack, and nutritionists recommend eating several portions each day. However, to discover its full glory it is worth spending a little time making a special dessert. Some, such as fresh fruit salads, can be ready in minutes. Others, such as sorbets and ice creams, take little time to prepare but do require time for freezing. Pies and tarts can be as elaborate or as simple as you like, and fruit also offers the cook an opportunity to make imaginative desserts for entertaining.

Fruit is immensely versatile; it is delicious served hot or cold and combines superbly with many other ingredients.

You are sure to find the ideal recipe for a really fruity dessert in this book, whether for a family supper, an informal lunch with friends or a sophisticated dinner party. Don't forget that recipes can often be varied using fruits in season – so enjoy the luscious flavours of fruit all year round.

Types of Fruit

The range of fruits available has never been so extensive, and new varieties are appearing all the time.

Apples & Pears

The most popular of all fruits, apples are perfect for eating raw or in hot or cold puddings. Available all year round there are many flavours and textures to choose from.

Apples

Sweet and juicy pears have a fine white flesh and are more often enjoyed raw than cooked.

Pears

Citrus Fruits

Lemons and limes are interchangeable in most recipes, but lime has a more aromatic, intense flavour. Grapefruit may have green, yellow or pink-flushed skin, with yellow, green or pink flesh. Kumquats are tiny relatives of oranges and can be eaten whole, either raw or cooked. Oranges, satsumas, tangerines, clementines and numerous other small varieties of citrus fruits are virtually interchangeable.

Lemons

Oranges

Soft Fruits

The most popular are probably blackberries, blackcurrants, redcurrants, blueberries, raspberries and strawberries. Do not overlook cranberries. Although too sharp to eat raw, their intense flavour and stunning colour make them very good for cooking. Gooseberries for cooking are small, firm, green and quite sharp, while dessert varieties are larger and sweeter.

Strawberr

Stone Fruits

Apricots, peaches, plums and nectarines may be used raw or lightly poached. White peaches have the sweetest flavour and yellow varieties are more aromatic with a firmer texture. There are many dessert and cooking varieties of plums, ranging from pale gold to black. You can use slightly under-ripe plums for cooking. Sweet dessert cherries are available in the summer and have white, pink or black skins and a juicy flesh. Choose fruit that is firm and glossy.

Nectarines

Exotic Fruits

Bananas are the most familiar exotic fruit with a dense texture and sweet taste. Fresh dates are sweet and juicy and more succulent than dried. Physalis, or Cape gooseberries, are small, fragrant, pleasantly tart orange berries wrapped in a paper "cape". Fresh figs have green or purple skins and sweet, pinkish-red flesh. Available all year round, kiwi fruit need only peeling and slicing. Lychees are small with a hard pink skin and sweet-smelling, juicy flesh. The purplish brown skin of passion fruit is wrinkled when ripe. Cut the fruit in half and scoop out the juicy seeds. Pineapple, has juicy yellow flesh and is available all year. Star fruit falls into pretty five-pointed stars when sliced. The fruit is ripe when the

Dates

Kiwi Fruit

Passion Fruit

Star Fruit

Pineapples

edges begin to go brown. The skins of mangoes vary in colour, but the flesh should always be golden yellow, sweet and juicy. Pawpaws have smooth, yellow-orange skins when ripe. The flesh is orangey pink and similar in texture to a melon. Pomegranate seeds and pulp have a delicate, slightly tart flavour.

Mangoes

Pawpaws

Melons, Figs & Grapes

There are many varieties of melons from small sweet cantaloupes to large juicy red watermelons. Figs are delicious eaten fresh or dried. Black or green grapes are very popular for serving with cheese or in a fruit salad.

Watermelons

Fresh Figs

Grapes

Techniques

Peeling and Segmenting an Orange

1 Using a serrated knife, cut a thin slice from each end of the orange to expose the flesh. Cut off the peel, removing the white pith.

2 Hold the fruit over a bowl to catch the juice. Cut each segment between the membranes. Squeeze out the juice.

Peeling a Pineapple

1 Cut the pineapple across into slices of the desired thickness. Use a small, sharp knife to cut off the rind.

2 Hold each slice upright and cut out the "eyes". Remove the central core of each slice with an apple corer.

Preparing a Mango

1 Place the mango narrow side down on a chopping board. Cut off a thick lengthways slice, keeping the knife as close to the stone as possible. Turn the mango round and repeat on the other side. Cut off the flesh adhering to the stone and scoop out the flesh from the mango slices.

2 To make a "hedgehog", prepare the mango as above and score the flesh on each thick slice with criss-cross lines at 1 cm/½ in intervals, taking care not to cut through the skin.

3 Fold the mango halves inside out and serve.

4 When the mango is folded inside out, the cubes can be cut off using a sharp knife, if desired.

Freezing Berries

1 Open-freeze perfect specimens in a single layer on a baking sheet, then pack into rigid containers. Damaged berries can be puréed and sieved, then sweetened with sugar and frozen.

Peeling Stone Fruits

Fruits, such as peaches, nectarines and apricots, can be peeled with a sharp paring knife, but this may waste some of the delicious flesh. The following method removes the skin only.

Make a tiny nick in the skin. Cover with boiling water and leave for 15–30 seconds, depending on the ripeness of the fruit. Remove the fruit with a slotted spoon and peel off the skin, which should come away easily.

Removing Stones and Pips

To stone peaches, apricots etc, cut all round the fruit through the seam. Twist the halves in opposite directions, then lever out the stone with a knife.

• To stone cherries, put the fruit in a cherry stoner and push the bar into the fruit. The stone will be ejected.

• To remove grape pips, cut the grapes in half, then pick out the pips with the tip of a small sharp knife.

Cooked Fruit Purée

Fruit purées are a useful base for many desserts, and also make very good sauces for ice cream or tarts. They can be used immediately or left to cool and frozen for eating later.

1 Cook the fruit in a pan, with a small amount of water or sugar, until soft. If you use sugar alone, heat the fruit very gently, to prevent the sugar burning, until the fruit juice begins to run and the sugar dissolves.

2 Remove any stones from the fruit and then tip it into a food processor or blender and process until as smooth as desired. The mixture may then need to be sieved to achieve a velvety consistency.

Fresh Fruit with Mango Sauc

A salad made with fresh fruit is always refreshing and welcome, but it is especially delicious and attractive served with a puréed fruit sauce.

Serves 6

INGREDIENTS
1 large ripe mango, peeled, stoned
   and chopped
rind of 1 unwaxed orange
juice of 3 oranges
caster sugar, to taste
2 peaches
2 nectarines
1 small mango, peeled
2 plums
1 pear or ½ small melon
juice of 1 lemon
25–50 g/1–2 oz/2 heaped tbsp wild
   strawberries (optional)
25–50 g/1–2 oz/2 heaped tbsp raspberries
25–50 g/1–2 oz/2 heaped tbsp blueberries
small mint sprigs, to decorate

1 In a food processor fitted with the metal blade, process the large mango until smooth. Add the orange rind, juice and sugar to taste and process again until very smooth. Press through a sieve into a bowl and chill the sauce.

2 Peel the peaches, if liked, then sto: and slice the peaches, nectarines, mango and plums. Quarter the pear and remove the core or peel the melon, and slice thinly.

3 Place the sliced fruits on a large plate. Sprinkle with the lemon juice ar chill, covered with clear film, for up to 3 hours before serving. (Some fruits m. discolour if cut too far ahead of time.)

4 To serve, arrange the sliced fruits serving plates, spoon the berries on top, drizzle with a little mango sauce and decorate with mint sprigs. Serve the remaining sauce separately.

Fragrant Fruit Salad

The syrup of this exotic fruit salad is flavoured and sweetened with lime and coffee liqueur. It can be prepared up to a day before serving.

Serves 6

INGREDIENTS
130 g/4½ oz/⅔ cup sugar
thinly pared rind and juice
   of 1 lime
60 ml/4 tbsp coffee liqueur, such as
   Tia Maria, Kahlúa or Toussaint
1 small pineapple
1 pawpaw
2 pomegranates
1 medium mango
2 passion fruits
fine strips of lime peel,
   to decorate

2 Using a sharp knife, cut the plume and stalk end from the pineapple. Pe thickly and cut the flesh into bite-siz pieces, discarding the woody central core. Add to the bowl.

1 Put the sugar and lime rind in a small saucepan with 150 ml/¼ pint/ ⅔ cup water. Heat gently until the sugar dissolves, then bring to the boil and simmer for 5 minutes. Leave to cool, then strain into a large serving bowl, discarding the lime rind. Stir in the lime juice and liqueur.

3 Cut the pawpaw in half and scoo out the seeds. Cut away the skin, the cut into chunks. Cut the pomegrana in half and scoop out the seeds. Brea into clusters and add to the bowl.

4 Cut the mango lengthways, along each side of the stone. Peel the skin off the flesh and cut into chunks. Ad with the rest of the fruit to the bowl Stir well.

5 Halve the passion fruits and scoop out the flesh using a teaspoon. Spoon over the salad and serve, decorated with fine strips of lime peel.

COOK'S TIP: To maximize the flavour of the fruit, allow the salad to stand at room temperature for an hour before serving.

Strawberry & Avocado Salad in Ginger & Orange Sauce

Avocado is more often treated as a vegetable, but in the Caribbean it is used as a fruit, which of course it is!

Serves 4

INGREDIENTS
2 firm ripe avocados
3 firm ripe bananas, sliced
12 fresh strawberries, halved,
    or cherries
juice of 1 large orange
shredded fresh root
    ginger (optional)

FOR THE GINGER SYRUP
50 g/2 oz fresh root
    ginger, chopped
900 ml/1½ pints/3¾ cups water
225 g/8 oz/1 cup
    demerara sugar
2 cloves

1 First make the ginger syrup; place the ginger, water, sugar and cloves in a saucepan and bring to the boil. Reduce the heat and simmer for about 1 hour, until well reduced and syrupy.

2 Remove the ginger and discard. Leave to cool. Store in a covered container in the fridge.

3 Peel the avocados, cut into slices and place in a bowl with the bananas and strawberries or cherries.

COOK'S TIP: Avocados discolour when exposed to the air, so peel and slice them quickly. The orange juice and ginger syrup will prevent discolouration for some time.

4 Pour the orange juice over the
fruits. Add 60 ml/4 tbsp of the ginger
syrup and mix gently, using a metal
spoon. Chill for 30 minutes and add a
little shredded ginger, if liked.

Persian Melon

Called *Paludeh Garmac,* this is a typical Persian dessert using delicious, sweet fresh fruits flavoured with rose water and a hint of aromatic mint.

Serves 4

INGREDIENTS
2 small melons
225 g/8 oz/2 cups strawberries
3 peaches, peeled and cut into small cubes
1 bunch of seedless grapes (green or red)
30 ml/2 tbsp caster sugar
15 ml/1 tbsp rose water
15 ml/1 tbsp lemon juice
crushed ice (optional)
4 strawberries and sprigs of mint, to decorate

1 Cut the melons in half and remove the seeds. Scoop out the flesh with a melon baller, without damaging the skin. Reserve the melon shells. Alternatively, scoop out the flesh using a spoon and cut into bite-size pieces.

2 Reserve four strawberries and slice the others. Place in a bowl with the melon balls, the peaches, grapes, sugar, rose water and lemon juice.

3 Pile the fruit into the melon shells and chill in the fridge for 2 hours.

4 To serve, sprinkle with crushed ice if liked, decorating each melon with a whole strawberry and a sprig of mint.

VARIATION: If preferred, nectarines and raspberries could replace the peaches and strawberries.

Fruits of the Tropics Salad

Pineapple, guavas, bananas and mango are combined with ginger and coconut to make this exotic Caribbean dessert.

Serves 4–6

INGREDIENTS
1 medium pineapple
400 g/14 oz can guava halves
  in syrup
2 medium bananas, sliced
1 large mango, peeled, stoned
  and diced
115 g/4 oz stem ginger and
  30 ml/2 tbsp of the syrup
60 ml/4 tbsp thick coconut milk
10 ml/2 tsp sugar
2.5 ml/½ tsp freshly
  grated nutmeg
2.5 ml/½ tsp ground cinnamon
strips of coconut,
  to decorate

1 Peel, core and cube the pineapple, and place in a serving bowl. Drain the guavas, reserving the syrup, and chop. Add the guavas to the bowl with one of the bananas and the mango. Chop the stem ginger and add to the pineapple mixture.

2 Pour 30 ml/2 tbsp of the ginger syrup, and the reserved guava syrup into a blender or food processor and add the other banana, the coconut milk and the sugar. Process to make a smooth, creamy purée.

3 Pour the banana and coconut mixture over the fruit, add a little nutmeg and cinnamon. Serve chilled, decorated with strips of coconut.

Fresh Fruit Salad

Any fruits in season can be used for this salad.

Serves 6

INGREDIENTS
2 eating apples
2 oranges
2 peaches
16–20 strawberries
30 ml/2 tbsp lemon juice
15–30 ml/1–2 tbsp orange flower water
icing sugar, to taste
a few fresh mint leaves, to decorate

1 Peel, core and thinly slice the apples. Peel the oranges, removing all the pith, and segment them, catching any juice in a bowl.

2 Blanch the peaches for 1 minute in boiling water, then peel away the skin and cut the flesh into thick slices. Hull the strawberries and halve or quarter if large. Place all the fruit in a large serving bowl.

3 Blend together the lemon juice, orange flower water and any orange juice. Add a little icing sugar, if liked. Pour the fruit juice mixture over the fruit salad and serve decorated with mint leaves.

Right: Fresh Fruit Salad (top); Dried Fruit Salad

Dried Fruit Salad

This is a wonderful combination of fresh and dried fruits.

Serves 4

INGREDIENTS
115 g/4 oz/½ cup dried apricots
115 g/4 oz/½ cup dried peaches
1 fresh pear
1 fresh apple
1 fresh orange
115 g/4 oz/⅔ cup mixed raspberries
   and blackberries
1 cinnamon stick
50 g/2 oz/¼ cup caster sugar
15 ml/1 tbsp clear honey
30 ml/2 tbsp lemon juice

1 Soak the apricots and peaches in water for 1–2 hours, until plump, then drain and halve or quarter them.

2 Peel and core the pear and apple and cut into cubes. Peel the orange with a sharp knife, removing all the pith, and cut into wedges. Place all the fruit in a saucepan with the berries.

3 Add 600 ml/1 pint/2½ cups water, the cinnamon, sugar and honey and bring to the boil. Cover and simmer very gently for 10–12 minutes, then remove the pan from the heat. Stir in the lemon juice. Allow to cool, then pour into a serving bowl and chill for 1–2 hours before serving.

Blackberry Ice Cream

The sharpness of blackberries gives a delicious vibrancy to this superb and elegant ice cream. A delightful autumn dessert.

Serves 4–6

INGREDIENTS

500 g/1¼ lb/5 cups blackberries, hulled,
    plus extra, to decorate
75 g/3 oz/6 tbsp caster sugar
30 ml/2 tbsp water
300 ml/½ pint/1¼ cups
    whipping cream
crisp dessert biscuits,
    to serve

1 Put the blackberries, sugar and water into a saucepan. Cover and simmer for 5 minutes, until the berries are just soft.

2 Tip the fruit into a sieve placed over a bowl and press it through the mesh to purée. Leave to cool, then chill.

3 If you are using an ice cream maker, churn the purée for 10–15 minutes, until it is thick, then gradually pour in the cream. Continue to churn until it is firm enough to scoop.

4 If you are making the ice cream by hand, whip the cream until it is just thick but still soft enough to fall from a spoon, then mix it with the chilled purée. Pour into a freezerproof container and freeze for 2 hours.

5 Mash the mixture with a fork, or beat with an electric mixer to break up the ice crystals. Return it to the freezer for 4 hours more, beating the mixture again after 2 hours. Scoop into dishes and decorate with blackberries. Serve with biscuits.

Strawberry Semi Freddo

Serve this quick strawberry dessert semi-frozen to reap the full flavour.
Crisp dessert biscuits make the perfect accompaniment.

Serves 4–6

INGREDIENTS
250 g/9 oz/generous 2 cups strawberries
115 g/4 oz/generous ½ cup strawberry jam
250 g/9 oz/generous 1 cup ricotta cheese
200 g/7 oz/scant 1 cup Greek-style yogurt
5 ml/1 tsp vanilla essence
40 g/1½ oz/3 tbsp caster sugar
extra strawberries and mint or lemon balm,
   to decorate

1 Put the strawberries in a bowl and
mash them with a fork until broken
into small pieces but not completely
puréed. Stir in the jam.

2 Drain off any whey from the
ricotta. Tip it into a bowl and stir in
the yogurt, vanilla essence and sugar.

3 Using a dessertspoon, fold the
mashed strawberries into the ricotta
mixture until rippled.

4 Spoon into individual freezerproof
dishes and freeze for at least 2 hours,
until almost solid. Alternatively, freeze
until completely solid, then transfer
the ice cream to the fridge for about
45 minutes to soften before serving.
Serve with extra strawberries and mint
or lemon balm.

COOK'S TIPS: Don't mash the
strawberries too much or they will
liquefy. Freeze in a large freezer
container if you don't have suitable
small dishes. Transfer to the fridge to
thaw slightly, then scoop into glasses.

Peach & Cardamom Yogurt Ice

This unusual peach ice cream spiced with cardamom uses yogurt to provide a creamy, velvety texture.

Serves 4

INGREDIENTS
8 cardamom pods
6 peaches, total weight about 500 g/1¼ lb, halved, and stoned
75 g/3 oz/6 tbsp caster sugar
30 ml/2 tbsp water
200 ml/7 fl oz/scant 1 cup natural live yogurt

1 Put the cardamom pods on a board and crush them with the base of a ramekin, or use a mortar and pestle.

2 Chop the peaches roughly and put them in a saucepan. Add the crushed cardamom pods and seeds, the sugar and water. Cover and simmer for 10 minutes or until tender. Cool.

3 Tip the peach mixture into a food processor or blender, process until smooth, then press through a sieve placed over a bowl. If you are using an ice cream maker, churn the purée until thick, then scrape it into a freezerproof container. Stir in the yogurt and freeze until firm enough to scoop.

4 If you are making the ice cream by hand, sieve the peach purée into a bowl and stir in the yogurt. Pour the mixture into a plastic tub and freeze for 5–6 hours until firm, beating once or twice with a fork, electric mixer or in a food processor to break up the ice crystals. Scoop on to a large platter, or use a melon baller to make miniature scoops in individual dishes. Serve at once.

Mango & Orange Sorbet

Fresh and tangy, and gloriously vibrant in colour, this sorbet is the perfect finale for a spicy meal.

Serves 2–4

INGREDIENTS
115 g/4 oz/generous ½ cup golden
    caster sugar
2 large mangoes
juice of 1 orange
1 egg white (optional)
thinly pared strips of fresh
    unwaxed orange rind,
    to decorate

1 Gently heat the golden caster sugar and 300 ml/½ pint/1¼ cups water in a pan until the sugar has dissolved. Bring to the boil, then reduce the heat and simmer for 5 minutes. Leave to cool.

2 Cut away the two sides of the mango close to the stone. Peel, then cut the flesh from the stone. Dice the fruit. Process the mango flesh and orange juice in a food processor with the sugar syrup until smooth.

3 Pour the mixture into a freezerproof container and freeze for 2 hours until semi-frozen. Whisk the egg white, if using, until it forms stiff peaks, then stir it into the sorbet. Whisk well to remove any ice crystals and freeze until solid.

4 Transfer the sorbet to the fridge 10 minutes before serving. Serve, decorated with orange rind.

Iced Pear Terrine with Calvados & Chocolate Sauce

This terrine, based on a classic French dessert, makes a refreshing and impressive end to any meal. For flavour, be sure the pears are fully ripe.

Serves 8

INGREDIENTS
1.5 kg/3–3½ lb ripe Williams pears
juice of 1 lemon
115 g/4 oz/generous ½ cup caster sugar
10 whole cloves
90 ml/6 tbsp water
julienne strips of unwaxed orange rind,
    to decorate

FOR THE SAUCE
200 g/7 oz plain chocolate
60 ml/4 tbsp hot strong black coffee
200 ml/7 fl oz/scant 1 cup
    double cream
30 ml/2 tbsp Calvados
    or brandy

2 Process the pears with their juice in a food processor or blender until smooth. Pour the purée into a freezerproof bowl, cover and freeze until firm.

3 Meanwhile, line a 900 g/2 lb loaf tin with clear film. Allow the film to overhang the sides. Spoon the frozen pear purée into a food processor or blender. Process until smooth. Pour into the prepared tin, cover and freeze until firm.

1 Peel, core and slice the pears. Place them in a saucepan with the lemon juice, sugar, cloves and water. Cover and simmer for 10 minutes. Remove the cloves. Allow the pears to cool.

4 Make the sauce. Break the chocolate into a large heatproof bowl set over a saucepan of hot water. When the chocolate has melted, stir in the coffee until smooth. Gradually stir in the cream and then the Calvados or brandy. Set the sauce aside.

5 About 20 minutes before serving, remove the tin from the freezer. Invert the terrine on to a plate, lift off the clear film and place the terrine in the fridge to soften slightly. Warm the sauce over hot water. Place a slice of terrine on each dessert plate and spoon over some of the sauce. Decorate with julienne strips of orange rind and serve at once.

Currant Apple Mousse

This Romanian recipe uses crisp apples and currants, macerated in red wine, to make a creamy mousse.

Serves 4–6

INGREDIENTS
175 g/6 oz/¾ cup currants
175 ml/6 fl oz/¾ cup red wine,
    plus a little extra for topping up
4 crisp eating apples, cored,
    peeled and sliced
250 ml/8 fl oz/1 cup water
225 g/8 oz/generous 1 cup caster sugar
30 ml/2 tbsp cornflour
few drops of pink food
    colouring (optional)
3 egg yolks
5 ml/1 tsp vanilla essence
2.5 ml/½ tsp cinnamon
2 egg whites
seedless black grapes, a little caster sugar
    and mint leaves to decorate

1 Soak the currants in the red wine for 1–1½ hours. Drain and set aside. Strain the wine through a fine sieve, then top up with more wine as necessary to bring back up to 175 ml/ 6 fl oz/¾ cup.

2 Meanwhile, put the apples in a pan and cook with the water and three-quarters of the sugar until soft. Cool, then process the apples in a food processor and return the purée to the pan.

3 Blend together the cornflour and red wine and pour it into the purée. Cook for 8–10 minutes, stirring constantly. Add the food colouring, if using.

4 Beat the egg yolks in a bowl with the remaining sugar and the vanilla essence until pale and thick. Whisk the apple mixture slowly into the egg yolks. Add the cinnamon and beat until smooth.

5 Chill until thickened. Reserve 5 ml/ 1 tsp of the egg white for decorating and whisk the remainder until stiff. Fold the currants and the whisked egg whites into the apple mixture, pour into glasses and chill.

6 Meanwhile, make the frosted grapes. Brush the black grapes with a little of the reserved egg white and sprinkle with caster sugar. Leave to dry. Use with the mint leaves to decorate the mousse, and serve.

Cold Mango Soufflés Topped with Toasted Coconut

Fragrant, fresh mango is one of the most delicious exotic fruits around, whether it is simply served in slices or used as the basis for an ice cream or soufflé, as here.

Serves 4

INGREDIENTS
4 small mangoes, peeled, stoned
   and chopped
30 ml/2 tbsp water
15 ml/1 tbsp powdered gelatine
2 egg yolks
115 g/4 oz/generous ½ cup caster sugar
120 ml/4 fl oz/½ cup milk
grated rind of 1 unwaxed orange
300 ml/½ pint/1¼ cups
   double cream
toasted flaked or coarsely shredded
   coconut, to decorate

1 Place a few pieces of mango in the base of each of four 150 ml/¼ pint/ ⅔ cup ramekins. Wrap a greased collar of non-stick baking paper around the outside of each dish, extending well above the rim. Secure with adhesive tape, then tie tightly with string.

2 Pour the water into a small heatproof bowl and sprinkle the powdered gelatine on the surface. Leave for 5 minutes, or until spongy. Place the bowl in a pan of hot water, stirring occasionally, until the gelatine has dissolved.

3 Meanwhile, whisk the egg yolks with the caster sugar and milk in another heatproof bowl. Place the bowl over a saucepan of simmering water and continue to whisk until the mixture is thick and frothy. Remove from the heat and continue whisking until the mixture cools. Whisk in the liquid gelatine.

4 Process the remaining mango in a food processor or blender, then fold the purée into the egg yolk mixture with the orange rind. Set the mixture aside until starting to thicken.

5 Whip the double cream to soft peaks. Reserve 60 ml/4 tbsp and fold the rest into the mango mixture. Spoon into the ramekins until the mixture is 2.5 cm/1 in above the rim of each dish. Chill for 3–4 hours, or until the mixture is set.

6 Carefully remove the paper collars from the soufflés. Spoon a little of the reserved cream on top of each soufflé and decorate with some toasted flaked or coarsely shredded coconut.

Orange-blossom Jelly

This natural fruit jelly has a cleansing quality that is welcome after a rich main course. Decorate it with edible flowers, if desired.

Serves 4–6

INGREDIENTS
65 g/2½ oz/5 tbsp caster sugar
150 ml/¼ pint/⅔ cup water
2 sachets of powdered gelatine
  (about 25 g/1 oz)
600 ml/1 pint/2½ cups freshly squeezed
  orange juice
30 ml/2 tbsp orange flower water

1 Place the caster sugar and water in a small saucepan and gently heat to dissolve the sugar, stirring occasionally. Leave to cool.

2 Sprinkle over the gelatine, ensuring it is completely submerged in the water. Leave to stand until the gelatine has absorbed all the liquid and is solid.

3 Gently melt the gelatine over a bowl of simmering water until it becomes clear and transparent. Leave to cool. When the gelatine is cold, mix it with the orange juice and orange flower water.

4 Wet a jelly mould and pour in the jelly. Chill in the refrigerator for at least 2 hours, or until set. Turn out to serve.

Apple Mint & Pink Grapefruit Fool

Besides looking particularly attractive, pink grapefruit is usually slightly less tart than the yellow varieties.

Serves 4–6

INGREDIENTS
500 g/1¼ lb tart apples, peeled and sliced
225 g/8 oz pink grapefruit segments
45 ml/3 tbsp clear honey
30 ml/2 tbsp water
2 large sprigs of apple mint,
  plus extra to decorate
150 ml/¼ pint/⅔ cup double cream
300 ml/½ pint/1¼ cups custard

1 Place the apples, grapefruit, honey, water and apple mint in a pan, cover and simmer for 10 minutes until soft.

2 Leave in the pan to cool, then discard the apple mint. Process the mixture in a food processor.

3 Whip the double cream until it forms soft peaks, and fold into the custard. Carefully fold the custard cream into the apple and grapefruit mixture, reserving 30 ml/2 tbsp to decorate.

4 Pour into individual glasses. Chill, then decorate with swirls of the remaining custard cream and small sprigs of apple mint.

Passion Fruit Crème Caramels with Dipped Physalis

The aromatic flavour of passion fruit really permeates these delightful crèm caramels. Physalis are dipped in some of the caramel to create a unique decoration. These caramels will make an excellent dinner party dessert.

Serves 4

INGREDIENTS
185 g/6½ oz/scant 1 cup
   caster sugar
75 ml/5 tbsp water
4 passion fruit
4 physalis
3 eggs plus 1 egg yolk
150 ml/¼ pint/⅔ cup double cream
150 ml/¼ pint/⅔ cup
   creamy milk

2 Meanwhile, cut each passion fruit in half. Scoop out the seeds into a sieve set over a bowl. Press the seeds against the sieve to extract all their juice. Spoon a few of the seeds into each of four 150 ml/¼ pint/⅔ cup ramekins. Set the juice aside.

1 Place 150 g/5 oz/¾ cup of the caster sugar in a heavy-based saucepan. Add the water and heat gently until the sugar has dissolved. Increase the heat and boil until the syrup turns a dark golden colour.

COOK'S TIP Baking the custards in water stops them from curdling.

3 Peel back the papery casing from each physalis and dip the orange berries into the caramel. Place on a sheet of non-stick baking paper and set aside. Pour the remaining caramel carefully into the ramekins.

4 Preheat the oven to 150°C/300°F/ Gas 2. Whisk the eggs, egg yolk and remaining sugar in a bowl. Whisk in the cream and milk, then the passion fruit juice. Strain into each ramekin, then place the ramekins in a baking tin. Pour in hot water to come halfway up the sides of the dishes and bake for 40–45 minutes, or until just set.

5 Remove the custards from the tin and leave to cool, then cover and chill them for 4 hours before serving. Run a knife between the edge of each ramekin and the custard and invert each in turn on to a dessert plate. Shake the ramekins firmly to release the custards. Decorate each with a dipped physalis.

Jamaican Fruit Trifle

A deliciously light version of a traditional Caribbean dessert contains plenty of fruit and is made with crème fraîche, as well as cream.

Serves 8

INGREDIENTS

1 large sweet pineapple, peeled and cored, about 350 g/12 oz, leaves reserved
300 ml/½ pint/1¼ cups double cream
200 ml/7 fl oz/scant 1 cup crème fraîche
60 ml/4 tbsp icing sugar, sifted
10 ml/2 tsp vanilla essence
30 ml/2 tbsp white or coconut rum
3 pawpaws, peeled, seeded and chopped
3 mangoes, peeled, stoned and chopped
thinly pared rind and juice of 1 lime
25 g/1 oz/⅓ cup coarsely shredded or flaked coconut, toasted, (optional)

1 Cut the pineapple into large chunks, place in a food processor or blender and process briefly until chopped. Tip into a sieve placed over a bowl and leave for 5 minutes so that most of the juice drains from the fruit.

COOK'S TIP: It is important to allow the chopped pineapple to drain thoroughly, otherwise the pineapple cream will be watery. Don't throw away the drained pineapple juice – mix it with fizzy mineral water for a refreshing drink.

2 Whip the double cream to very soft peaks, then lightly but thoroughly fold in the crème fraîche, sifted icing sugar, vanilla essence and rum.

3 Fold the drained, chopped pineapple into the cream mixture. Place the chopped pawpaws and mangoes in a large bowl and pour over the lime juice. Gently stir the fruit mixture to combine. Shred the pared lime rind.

4 Divide the fruit mixture and the pineapple cream among eight dessert plates. Decorate with the lime shreds, toasted coconut, if using, and small pineapple leaves, and serve at once.

Apricot & Hazelnut Meringue Roll with Apricot Brandy

A soft nutty meringue, rolled around a creamy apricot filling spiked with apricot brandy makes a superb dinner party dessert.

Serves 6

INGREDIENTS
5 egg whites
150 g/5 oz/¾ cup caster sugar
5 ml/1 tsp cornflour
50 g/2 oz/½ cup toasted hazelnuts, chopped
icing sugar, for dusting
apricot slices and mint sprigs,
    to decorate

FOR THE FILLING
300 ml/½ pint/1¼ cups double cream
30 ml/2 tbsp apricot brandy
60 ml/4 tbsp apricot conserve, any large
    chunks chopped
6 apricots, stoned and thinly sliced

1 Preheat the oven to 110°C/225°F/ Gas ¼. Grease a 30 x 20 cm/12 x 8 in Swiss roll tin and line it with non-stick baking parchment. Whisk the egg whites until stiff but not dry. Whisk in half the sugar and then continue to whisk until the mixture is stiff. Fold in the remaining sugar.

VARIATION: You can add extra texture and flavour by turning the baked meringue on to a sheet of non-stick baking parchment dusted with ground hazelnuts.

2 Fold in the cornflour and hazelnuts and spoon the mixture into the tin. Bake for about 45 minutes, or until set. Leave the meringue in the tin to cool, uncovered, for 1 hour.

3 Whip the cream lightly in a bowl, then stir in the apricot brandy and conserve. Fold in the apricot slices.

4 Dust a sheet of non-stick baking parchment with icing sugar and turn the meringue on to it. Peel away the lining paper and spread the filling over the top of the meringue.

5 With the aid of the parchment, and working from a short end, roll the meringue over the filling. Place the roll on a serving plate, dust with more icing sugar and decorate with apricot slices and mint sprigs.

Raspberry Millefeuille

Succulent raspberries and luscious confectioner's custard are sandwiched between layers of melt-in-the-mouth puff pastry.

Serves 8

INGREDIENTS

450 g/1 lb rough-puff or puff pastry, thawed if frozen
6 egg yolks
65 g/2½ oz/⅓ cup caster sugar
45 ml/3 tbsp plain flour
350 ml/12 fl oz/1½ cups milk
30 ml/2 tbsp kirsch or cherry liqueur (optional)
450 g/1 lb/2⅔ cups raspberries
icing sugar, for dusting
strawberry or raspberry *coulis,* to serve

1 Lightly butter two large baking sheets and sprinkle them very lightly with cold water.

2 On a lightly floured surface, roll out the pastry to a 3 mm/⅛ in thickness. Using a 10 cm/4 in cutter, cut out 12 rounds. Place on the baking sheets and prick each a few times with a fork. Chill for 30 minutes. Preheat the oven to 200°C/400°F/Gas 6.

3 Bake the pastry rounds for about 15–20 minutes, until golden, then transfer to wire racks to cool.

4 Whisk the egg yolks and sugar for 2 minutes, until light and creamy, then whisk in the flour until just blended. Bring the milk to the boil over a medium heat and pour it over the egg mixture, whisking to blend.

5 Return to the saucepan, bring to the boil and boil for 2 minutes, whisking constantly. Remove the pan from the heat and whisk in the kirsch or liqueur if using. Pour into a bowl and press clear film on to the surface to prevent a skin forming. Set aside to cool.

COOK'S TIP: To make a raspberry or strawberry *coulis,* crush 225 g/8 oz/ 1¼ cups berries to a purée with a fork, then rub through a fine strainer set over a clean bowl with the back of a spoon. Sweeten with icing sugar.

6 Carefully split the pastry rounds in half. Spread one round at a time with a little custard. Arrange a layer of raspberries over the custard and top with a second pastry round. Spread with a little more custard and a few more raspberries. Top with a third pastry round flat-side up. Dust with icing sugar and serve with the *coulis*.

Coffee Pavlova with Exotic Fruits

You can use virtually any fruit in season to decorate the meringue base – let your imagination run riot.

Serves 6–8

INGREDIENTS
30 ml/2 tbsp ground coffee, e.g. mocha
30 ml/2 tbsp near-boiling water
3 egg whites
2.5 ml/½ tsp cream of tartar
175 g/6 oz/scant 1 cup
   caster sugar
5 ml/1 tsp cornflour, sifted

FOR THE FILLING
150 ml/¼ pint/⅔ cup
   double cream
5 ml/1 tsp orange flower water
150 ml/¼ pint/⅔ cup crème fraîche
500 g/1¼ lb sliced exotic fruits, such as
   mango, papaya and kiwi
15 ml/1 tbsp icing sugar, (optional)

1 Preheat the oven to 140°C/275°F/ Gas 1. Draw a 20 cm/8 in circle on non-stick baking parchment. Place pencil-side down on a baking sheet.

2 Put the coffee in a small bowl and pour the hot water over. Leave to infuse for 4 minutes, then strain through a very fine sieve.

3 Whisk the egg whites with the cream of tartar until stiff, but not dry. Gradually whisk in the sugar until the meringue is stiff and shiny, then quickly whisk in the cornflour and coffee.

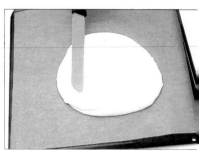

4 Using a long knife or spatula, spread the meringue mixture on to the prepared baking sheet to an even 20 cm/ 8 in round. Make a slight hollow in the middle. Bake in the oven for 1 hour, then turn off the heat and leave in the oven until cool.

VARIATION: 450g/1lb soft fruit, such as wild or cultivated strawberries, raspberries or blueberries, may be used instead of the exotic fruits.

5 Peel off the lining paper and transfer the meringue to a serving plate. To make the filling, whip the double cream with the orange flower water until soft peaks form. Fold in the crème fraîche. Spoon into the centre of the meringue. Arrange the exotic fruits over the cream and dust with icing sugar, if using.

Bananas with Lime & Cardamom Sauce

These delicious spiced bananas can also be served with folded crêpes.

Serves 6

INGREDIENTS
6 bananas
50 g/2 oz/ 4 tbsp butter
seeds from 4 cardamom pods, crushed
50 g/2 oz/½ cup flaked almonds
thinly pared rind and juice of 2 limes
50 g/2 oz/¼ cup light muscovado sugar
30 ml/2 tbsp dark rum
vanilla ice cream, to serve

1 Peel the bananas and cut them in half lengthways. Heat half the butter in a large frying pan. Add half the bananas, and cook until the undersides are golden. Turn carefully, using a fish slice. Cook until golden.

2 As they cook, transfer the bananas to a heatproof serving dish. Cook the remaining bananas in the same way.

3 Melt the remaining butter, then add the cardamom seeds and almonds. Cook, stirring until golden.

4 Stir in the lime rind and juice, then the sugar. Cook, stirring, until the mixture is smooth, bubbling and slightly reduced. Stir in the rum. Pour the sauce over the bananas and serve immediately, with vanilla ice cream.

VARIATION: If you prefer not to use alcohol in your cooking, replace the rum with fresh fruit juice.

Citrus Fruit Flambé with Pistachio Praline

Serves 4

INGREDIENTS

oil, for greasing
115 g/4 oz/generous ½ cup caster sugar
50 g/2 oz/½ cup pistachio nuts
2 oranges
1 ruby grapefruit
2 limes
50 g/2 oz/¼ cup butter
50 g/2 oz/¼ cup light muscovado sugar
45 ml/3 tbsp Cointreau
fresh mint sprigs, to decorate

1 Brush a baking sheet with oil. Place the sugar and nuts in a heavy-based saucepan and cook gently, swirling the pan, until the sugar has melted. Cook over a low heat until the nuts start to pop and the sugar has turned dark gold.

2 Pour on to the baking sheet and cool. Chop the praline into chunks.

3 Cut off the rind and pith from the citrus fruit. Cut between the membranes so that the segments fall into a bowl, with any juice.

4 Heat the butter and sugar in a heavy-based frying pan until the sugar has melted. Strain the citrus juices into the pan and cook, stirring occasionally, until reduced and syrupy.

5 Add the fruit segments and warm through without stirring. Pour over the Cointreau and set it alight. When the flames die down, spoon the flambé into serving dishes. Serve scattered with praline and decorated with mint.

Apple Soufflé Omelette

This delicious autumn filling is made by sautéing apples until they are slightly caramelized – you could use fresh berry fruits in the summer.

Serves 2

INGREDIENTS
4 eggs, separated
30 ml/2 tbsp single cream
15 ml/1 tbsp caster sugar
15 g/½ oz/1 tbsp butter
icing sugar, for dredging

FOR THE FILLING
1 eating apple, peeled, cored and sliced
25 g/1 oz/2 tbsp butter
30 ml/2 tbsp soft light brown sugar
45 ml/3 tbsp single cream

1 To make the filling, sauté the apple slices in the butter and sugar in a heavy-based pan over a low heat until just tender. Stir in the cream and keep warm, while making the omelette.

COOK'S TIP: When whisking egg whites, make sure that the bowl and whisk are both grease-free and that there is no yolk mixed in.

2 Place the egg yolks in a bowl with the cream and sugar and beat well. Whisk the egg whites until stiff, then fold into the yolk mixture using a figure-of-eight motion.

3 Melt the butter in a large, heavy-based frying pan, pour in the soufflé mixture evenly. Cook for 1 minute until golden underneath, then place under a hot grill to brown the top.

4 Slide the omelette on to a plate, add the apple mixture, then fold over Sift the icing sugar over thickly, then mark in a criss-cross pattern with a hot metal skewer. Serve immediately.

Peach & Raspberry Crumble

A quick and easy tasty dessert, this crumble is good served hot or cold, on its own, or with custard.

Serves 4

INGREDIENTS

75 g/3 oz/⅔ cup plain wholemeal flour
75 g/3 oz/¾ cup medium oatmeal
75 g/3 oz/6 tbsp butter
50 g/2 oz/¼ cup light brown sugar
2.5 ml/½ tsp ground cinnamon
400 g/14 oz can peach slices in fruit juice
225 g/8 oz/1⅓ cups raspberries
30 ml/2 tbsp clear honey
sprig of fresh mint, to garnish

1 Preheat the oven to 180°C/350°F/ Gas 4. Put the flour and oatmeal in a bowl and mix together.

2 Rub in the butter until the mixture resembles breadcrumbs, then stir in the sugar and cinnamon.

3 Drain the peach slices and reserve the juice. Chop the peach slices to about the same size as the raspberries.

4 Arrange the chopped peaches evenly over the base of an ovenproof dish, then scatter over the raspberries.

5 Mix together the reserved peach juice and honey, pour the mixture over the fruit and stir.

VARIATION: For a tasty change, use other combinations of fruit, such as apples and blackberries, rhubarb and orange, or strawberries and pineapple. If using all fresh fruit, add a little fruit juice.

6 Spoon the crumble mixture over the fruit, pressing it down lightly. Bake for about 45 minutes, until golden brown on top. Garnish with fresh mint and serve hot or cold.

Apricot Panettone Pudding

Slices of light-textured panettone are layered with dried apricots and cooked in a creamy coffee custard for a satisfyingly warming dessert.

Serves 4

INGREDIENTS

50 g/2 oz/4 tbsp unsalted butter, softened
6 x 1 cm/½ in thick slices (about 400 g/
    14 oz) panettone containing candied fruit
175 g/6 oz/¾ cup ready-to-eat dried
    apricots, chopped
400 ml/14 fl oz/1⅔ cups milk
250 ml/8 fl oz/1 cup double cream
60 ml/4 tbsp mild-flavoured
    ground coffee
90 g/3½ oz/½ cup caster sugar
3 eggs
30 ml/2 tbsp demerara sugar
pouring cream or crème fraîche,
    to serve

1 Preheat the oven to 160°C/325°F/ Gas 3. Brush a 2 litre/3½ pint/8 cup oval ovenproof dish with 15 g/½ oz/ 1 tbsp of the butter. Spread the panettone with the remaining butter and arrange in the dish. Cut to fit, and scatter the apricots among and over the layers.

2 Pour the milk and cream into a pa and heat until almost boiling. Pour th milk mixture over the coffee and lea to infuse for 10 minutes. Strain through a fine sieve, discarding the coffee grounds.

3 Lightly beat the caster sugar and eggs together, then whisk in the war coffee-flavoured milk. Slowly pour th mixture over the panettone. Leave to soak for 15 minutes.

4 Sprinkle the top of the pudding with demerara sugar and place the di in a large roasting tin. Pour in enoug boiling water to come halfway up the sides of the dish.

5 Bake for 40–45 minutes, until the top is golden and crusty, but the middle still slightly wobbly. Remove from the oven, but leave the dish in the hot water for 10 minutes. Serve the pudding warm with pouring cream or crème fraîche.

Coffee Crêpes with Peaches & Cream

Juicy golden peaches and cream conjure up the sweet taste of summer.
Here they are delicious as the filling for these light coffee crêpes.

Serves 6

INGREDIENTS
75 g/3 oz/⅔ cup plain flour
25 g/1 oz/¼ cup buckwheat flour
1.5 ml/¼ tsp salt
1 egg, beaten
200 ml/7 fl oz/scant 1 cup milk
15 g/½ oz/1 tbsp butter, melted
100 ml/3½ fl oz/scant ½ cup strong
   brewed coffee, strained
sunflower oil, for frying

FOR THE FILLING
6 ripe peaches
300 ml/½ pint/1¼ cups double cream
15 ml/1 tbsp amaretto liqueur
225 g/8 oz/1 cup mascarpone cheese
65 g/2½ oz/5 tbsp caster sugar
30 ml/2 tbsp icing sugar, for dusting (optional)

1 Sift the flours and salt into a mixing
bowl. Make a well in the middle and
add the egg, half the milk and the
melted butter. Gradually mix in the
flour, beating until smooth, then beat
in the remaining milk and coffee.

COOK'S TIP: To keep the pancakes
warm while you make the rest, cover
them with foil and place the plate
over a pan of barely simmering water.

2 Heat a drizzle of oil in a 15–20 cm/
6–8 in crêpe pan. Pour in just enough
batter to cover the base of the pan.
Cook for 2–3 minutes, until the
underneath is golden brown, then flip
over and cook the other side.

3 Slide the crêpe out of the pan on
to a plate. Continue making crêpes in
this way until all the mixture is used,
stacking and interleaving with
greaseproof paper.

To make the filling, halve the peaches and remove the stones. Cut into thick slices. Whip the cream and amaretto liqueur until soft peaks form. Beat the mascarpone with the sugar until smooth. Beat 30 ml/2 tbsp of the cream into the mascarpone, then fold in the remainder.

5 Spoon a little of the amaretto cream on to one half of each pancake and top with peach slices. Gently fold the pancake over and dust with icing sugar, if desired. Serve immediately.

51

Fresh Fig Filo Tart

Figs cook wonderfully well and taste superb in this tart – the riper the figs, the better they will taste.

Serves 6–8

INGREDIENTS

five 35 x 25 cm/14 x 10 in sheets filo pastry,
    thawed if frozen
25 g/1 oz/2 tbsp butter, melted, plus extra,
    for greasing
6 fresh figs, cut into wedges
75 g/3 oz/²⁄₃ cup plain flour
75 g/3 oz/6 tbsp caster sugar
4 eggs
450 ml/¾ pint/scant 2 cups creamy milk
2.5 ml/½ tsp almond essence
15 ml/1 tbsp icing sugar, for dusting
whipped cream or Greek-style yogurt,
    to serve

1 Preheat the oven to 190°C/375°F/
Gas 5. Grease a 25 x 16 cm/10 x 6¼ in
baking tin with butter. Brush each filo
sheet in turn with melted butter and
use to line the prepared tin.

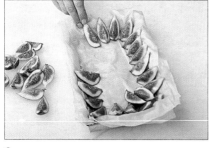

2 Using scissors, cut off any excess
pastry, leaving a little overhanging the
edge. Arrange the figs in the filo case.

3 Sift the flour into a bowl and stir in
the caster sugar. Add the eggs and a
little of the milk and whisk until
smooth. Gradually whisk in the
remaining milk and the almond
essence. Pour the mixture over the figs
and bake for 1 hour, or until the batter
has set and is golden.

4 Remove the tart from the oven and
allow it to cool in the tin on a wire
rack for 10 minutes. Remove from the
tin, if you like. Dust with the icing
sugar and serve with whipped cream
or Greek-style yogurt.

Exotic Fruit Tranche

This is a good way to make the most of a small selection of exotic fruit and looks simply amazing.

Serves 8

INGREDIENTS
175 g/6 oz/1½ cups plain flour
50 g/2 oz/¼ cup unsalted butter
25 g/1 oz/2 tbsp white vegetable fat
50 g/2 oz/¼ cup caster sugar
2 egg yolks
about 15 ml/1 tbsp cold water
115 g/4 oz/scant ½ cup apricot conserve,
  sieved and warmed

FOR THE FILLING
150 ml/¼ pint/⅔ cup double cream,
  plus extra to serve
250 g/9 oz/generous 1 cup
  mascarpone cheese
25 g/1 oz/¼ cup icing sugar, sifted
grated rind of 1 unwaxed orange
450 g/1 lb/3 cups mixed prepared fruits,
  such as mango, pawpaw, star fruit,
  kiwi fruit and blackberries
90 ml/6 tbsp apricot conserve, sieved
  and 15 ml/1 tbsp white or coconut
  rum, to glaze

1 Sift the flour into a bowl and rub in the butter and white vegetable fat until the mixture resembles fine breadcrumbs. Stir in the caster sugar. Add the egg yolks and enough cold water to make a soft dough.

2 Thinly roll out the pastry between two sheets of clear film and use the pastry to line a 35 x 12 cm/14 x 4½ in fluted tranche tin. Allow the excess pastry to hang over the edge of the tin and chill for 30 minutes.

3 Preheat the oven to 200°C/400°F/Gas 6. Prick the base of the pastry case with a fork, and line with non-stick baking paper and baking beans. Bake for 10–12 minutes.

4 Lift out the paper and beans and return the pastry case to the oven for 5 minutes. Trim off the excess pastry and brush the inside of the case with the warmed apricot conserve to form a seal. Leave to cool on a wire rack.

5 Make the filling. Whip the double cream to soft peaks, then stir it into the mascarpone with the icing sugar and orange rind. Spread the mixture inside the cooled pastry case and top with the prepared fruits.

6 Warm the remaining apricot conserve with the rum, and drizzle or brush over the fruits to make a glaze. Serve the tranche with extra cream.

VARIATION: If you don't have a tranche tin, line a 23 cm/9 in flan tin with the pastry.

Pear & Blueberry Pie

Bursting with fruit and full of flavour, this double-crust pie is the perfect choice for a family supper.

Serves 4

INGREDIENTS
225 g/8 oz/2 cups plain flour
pinch of salt
50 g/2 oz/¼ cup lard, cubed
50 g/2 oz/¼ cup butter, cubed
675 g/1½ lb/5 cups blueberries
30 ml/2 tbsp caster sugar
15 ml/1 tbsp arrowroot
2 ripe, but firm, pears, peeled,
    cored and sliced
2.5 ml/½ tsp ground cinnamon
grated rind of ½ unwaxed lemon
beaten egg, to glaze
caster sugar, for sprinkling
crème fraîche, to serve

1 Sift the flour and salt into a bowl and rub in the lard and butter until the mixture resembles fine breadcrumbs. Stir in 45 ml/3 tbsp cold water and mix to a dough. Chill for 30 minutes.

2 Place 225 g/8 oz/2 cups of the blueberries in a pan with the sugar. Cover and cook gently until the blueberries have softened. Press through a nylon sieve to remove the seeds.

3 Blend the arrowroot with 30 ml/ 2 tbsp cold water and add to the blueberry purée. Bring to the boil, stirring until thickened. Cool slightly.

4 Place a baking sheet in the oven and preheat to 190°C/375°F/Gas 5. Roll out just over half the pastry on a lightly floured surface and use to line a 20 cm/8 in shallow pie dish or plate.

5 Mix together the remaining blueberries, the pears, cinnamon and lemon rind and spoon into the dish. Pour the blueberry purée over the top.

6 Roll out the remaining pastry and use to cover the pie. Make a small slit in the centre. Brush with egg and sprinkle with caster sugar. Bake the pie on the hot baking sheet, for 40–45 minutes, until golden. Serve warm with crème fraîche.

Fresh Lemon Tart

This refreshing tart should be served at room temperature if the zesty lemon flavour is to be enjoyed to the full.

Serves 6–8

INGREDIENTS
350 g/12 oz ready-made rich sweet
   shortcrust pastry, thawed if frozen

FOR THE FILLING
3 eggs
115 g/4 oz/generous ½ cup
   caster sugar
115 g/4 oz/1 cup ground almonds
105 ml/7 tbsp double cream
grated rind and juice of
   2 unwaxed lemons

FOR THE TOPPING
2 thin-skinned unwaxed lemons,
   thinly sliced
200 g/7 oz/1 cup caster sugar
105 ml/7 tbsp water

1 Roll out the pastry and use it to line a deep 23 cm/9 in fluted flan tin. Prick the base with a fork and chill for 30 minutes.

2 Preheat the oven to 200°C/400°F/ Gas 6. Line the pastry with non-stick baking paper and baking beans and bake blind for 10 minutes. Remove the paper and beans and return the pastry case to the oven for 5 minutes more.

3 Meanwhile, make the filling. Beat the eggs, caster sugar, almonds and cream in a bowl until smooth. Beat in the lemon rind and juice. Pour the filling into the pastry case. Lower the oven temperature to 190°C/375°F/ Gas 5 and bake for 20 minutes or until the filling has set and the pastry is lightly golden.

4 Make the topping. Place the lemon slices in a pan and pour over water to cover. Simmer for 15–20 minutes, or until the skins are tender, then drain.

VARIATION: If you prefer not to candy the lemons, simply dust the tart with icing sugar.

5 Place the sugar in a saucepan and stir in the measured water. Heat gently until the sugar has dissolved, stirring constantly, then boil for 2 minutes. Add the lemon slices and cook for 10–15 minutes, until the skins become shiny and candied.

6 Lift out the candied lemon slices and arrange them over the top of the tart. Return the syrup to the heat and boil until reduced to a thick glaze. Brush this over the tart and allow to cool completely before serving, but do not chill.

59

Cherry Strudel

While quite time-consuming to make, cherry strudel, with its light-as-air texture and fruity filling, is well worth the effort.

Serves 8–10

INGREDIENTS
250 g/9 oz/2¼ cups strong plain flour
75 g/3 oz/⅔ cup plain flour
1 egg, beaten
150 g/5 oz/10 tbsp butter, melted
100 ml/3½ fl oz/scant ½ cup warm water
sifted icing sugar, for dredging

FOR THE FILLING
65 g/2½ oz/generous ½ cup walnuts,
   roughly chopped
115 g/4 oz/generous ½ cup caster sugar
675 g/1½ lb cherries, stoned
40 g/1½ oz/¾ cup day-old
   breadcrumbs

1 Preheat the oven to 200°C/400°F/ Gas 6. Sift the flours together into a warm bowl. Make a well in the centre, add the egg, 115 g/4 oz/½ cup of the melted butter and the water. Mix to a smooth, pliable dough, adding a little extra flour if required. Leave wrapped in clear film for 30 minutes to rest.

2 Meanwhile, in a large bowl, mix together the chopped walnuts, sugar, cherries and breadcrumbs.

3 Lay out a clean dish towel and sprinkle it with flour. Carefully roll out the dough until it covers the towel. The dough should be as thin as possible, so that you can see the design on the cloth through it.

4 Dampen the edges with water. Spread the cherry filling over the pastry, leaving a gap all the way around the edge, about 2.5 cm/1 in wide. Roll up the pastry carefully with the side edges folded in over the filling to prevent it from coming out. Use the dish towel to help you roll the pastry.

5 Brush the strudel with the remaining melted butter. Place on a baking sheet and curl into a horseshoe shape. Cook for 30–40 minutes, or until golden brown. Dredge with icing sugar and serve warm or cold.

Upside-down Apple Tart

A special *tarte tatin* – the original French name of this dish – tin is ideal, but an ovenproof frying pan will do very well.

Serves 8–10

INGREDIENTS
225 g/8 oz puff or shortcrust pastry, thawed
   if frozen
10–12 large Golden Delicious apples
lemon juice
115 g/4 oz/½ cup butter, cut into pieces
115 g/4 oz/generous ½ cup caster sugar
2.5 ml/½ tsp ground cinnamon
crème fraîche or whipped cream,
   to serve

1 On a lightly floured surface, roll out the pastry into a 28 cm/11 in round less than 5 mm/¼ in thick. Transfer to a lightly floured baking sheet and chill.

2 Peel the apples, cut them in half lengthways and core. Sprinkle the apples generously with lemon juice.

3 In a 25 cm/10 in *tarte tatin* tin, cook the butter, sugar and cinnamon over a medium heat until the butter has melted and the sugar has dissolved, stirring occasionally.

4 Continue cooking for 6–8 minutes, until the mixture turns a medium caramel colour, then remove the tin from the heat and arrange the apple halves, standing on their edges, in the tin, fitting them in tightly since they shrink during cooking.

5 Return the apple-filled tin to the heat and bring to a simmer over a medium heat for 20–25 minutes, until the apples are tender and coloured. Remove the tin from the heat and cool slightly.

6 Preheat the oven to 230°C/450°F/ Gas 8. Place the pastry on top of the apple-filled tin and tuck the edges of the pastry inside the edge of the tin around the apples. Pierce the pastry in two or three places, then bake for 25–30 minutes, until the pastry is golden and the filling is bubbling. Leave to cool in the tin for 10–15 minutes.

7 To serve, run a sharp knife around edge of the tin to loosen the pastry. Cover with a serving plate and, holding them tightly, carefully invert the tin and plate together (do this carefully, preferably over the sink in case any caramel drips). Lift off the tin and loosen any apples that stick with a palette knife. Serve warm with cream.

This paperback edition published in 2000 by Hermes House
an imprint of
Anness Publishing Limited
Hermes House
88-89 Blackfriars Road
London SE1 8HA

A CIP catalogue record for this book is available from the British Library

Publisher: Joanna Lorenz
Editor: Valerie Ferguson
Series Designer: Bobbie Colgate Stone
Designer: Andrew Heath
Editorial Reader: Marion Wilson
Production Controller: Joanna King

Recipes contributed by: Catherine Atkinson, Carole Clements, Trisha Davies, Nicola Diggins, Joanna
Farrow, Shirley Gill, Rosamund Grant, Sarah Lewis, Maggie Mayhew, Norma Miller, Katherine Richmond,
Anne Sheasby, Liz Trigg, Elizabeth Wolf-Cohen.

Photography: Karl Adamson, William Adams-Lingwood, Louise Dare, John Freeman, Michelle Garrett,
Ian Garlick, Amanda Heywood, Janine Hosegood, David Jordan, Patrick McLeavey, Thomas Odulate.

1 3 5 7 9 10 8 6 4 2

Notes:
For all recipes, quantities are given in both metric and imperial measures and, where appropriate,
measures are also given in standard cups
and spoons.
Follow one set, but not a mixture, because they are not interchangeable.

Standard spoon and cup measures are level.

1 tsp = 5 ml   1 tbsp = 15 ml

1 cup = 250 ml/8 fl oz

Australian standard tablespoons are 20 ml.
Australian readers should use 3 tsp in place of
1 tbsp for measuring small quantities of gelatine, cornflour, salt, etc.

Medium eggs are used unless otherwise stated.

Printed and bound in China